ACTS 3

ENVIRONMENT

THE ACTS OF THEN ARE THE ACTS OF NOW

PETER WIEBE

Scripture quotations taken from the (NASB ®) NEW AMERICAN STANDARD BIBLE ® , Copyright © 1960, 1971, 1977, 1995 by The Lockman Foundation. Used by permission. All rights reserved. www.lockman.org

ISBN: 978-1-7369924-0-1

Printed in the United States of America

"You want to be found reading your Bible because you love Jesus, not so you can argue better. "

- Peter Wiebe

CONTENTS

1

PRAYER

"Now Peter and John were going up to the temple at the ninth hour, the hour of prayer."
Acts 3:1

Everything in Acts chapter three began with the boys heading to prayer! They never even made it to the prayer meeting before they already saw a miracle!

Ultimately, the dedication of others *to pray* was a vital key to the lame man receiving his healing, and to all the events that followed.

Prayer is yielding to the Lord, finding out what He has to say, and what He would have us do. It is giving Him our attention. As you pray, He may ask you to make a change, or may correct your thinking, or warn you about a person or situation. Prayer is like a daily intelligence briefing. In combat, intelligence information is of highest importance! "What are we doing today, Lord?"

In 2016, I was way out on a ranch checking barbed wire fencing when the Lord began talking to me about how to pray for people. I knew immediately He was speaking of situations I would encounter in the future. He strongly impressed on me that I would regularly come across many people who need prayer. He instructed me to pray and release my faith according to Mark 11:24 over all the prayer needs I would be met with any given day, *before* that day is over. Don't wait until the next day or a later time. Once you've released your faith for their needs, believing that you have received what you've asked for, you don't need to drag yesterday's prayers into today by praying them again. This way you can start each new day fresh, focused, and forward facing.

TESTIMONY

Back when I was living as a bachelor in west Texas, a foreign exchange student I had briefly gotten to know came to my house one day. She had become extremely self-conscious of her appearance and was starving herself. Her other friends said she was already so weak and tired that all she wanted to do was sleep. Her hair was falling out, and all she ate was a little watermelon once in a while. As she was about to leave, standing on the porch I said, "I will pray for you." She didn't seem to be a very spiritual person, so it was like what I said kinda just went over her head. As soon as she left the house, I went to my room, knelt down, and prayed for her. That same evening I left for the weekend to my parents' house an hour away. I never locked my doors, and when I returned home two days later, I found she had left a two page letter on my bed. She wrote that within a day after I told her I would pray, "Suddenly something just TOLD ME TO EAT!" She was so excited, listing at least three things she had eaten and stating how good she felt! As a result of this supernatural answer to prayer, she acknowledged God and gave Him thanks!

2

HEALED INSTEAD

"When he saw Peter and John about to go into the temple, he began asking to receive alms. But Peter, along with John, fixed his gaze on him and said, 'Look at us!' And he began to give them his attention, expecting to receive something from them."
Acts 3:3-5

That day, the lame man learned he was mistaken in looking only for money or food! A burrito or some cash would have been entirely temporary. Healed and whole was infinitely better than a short term fix!

The Lord is always after us being whole in every area, not just sorta getting by in one or two areas.

The greatest gift you can give anyone is *you* being whole.

A trailer manufacturer in the area we used to live decided to replace their older, smaller security fence with a new one. During the space of time between tearing out the old and installing the new, they created a temporary, makeshift fence with their trailers parked end to end around the perimeter of the property. However, I guess one of those trailers got sold, so it was removed, and now there was a big gap in the "fence" where anyone could drive through to steal a trailer or anything else off the property. Just because *one* trailer was missing.

So you see, if not *whole*, there are still *holes*, where the enemy can come in to steal from you.

Not only did He want him made whole simply for the sake of wholeness, God's aim here was also for the lame man to be healed so he could go to work and fulfill his own God-given assignment, rather than relying solely on others for his supply.

There is a false supply and a true supply. Jeremiah 17:5-6 says those who put their trust in and look only to people as their source of supply will inevitably come to lack. It's a false supply. Then in verses 7-8 we see that those who put their trust in God as their source will always have a true and reliable supply!

In Scripture, we find that supply from the Lord can come in various ways, including by inheritance, working your gift, sowing and reaping, and the wealth of the wicked being transferred to the righteous. In all of these, it is vital to understand that He is the Source!

TESTIMONY

Around 2010 - 2011, I had been jogging two to five miles, sometimes several times a week, for about thirteen years. One day as I went to jog I suddenly had such severe pain in the side of my knee that I couldn't run. I tried multiple more times to go jogging, but couldn't because of the pain. I never told anyone, even my wife, because I believed the Word that I was healed and I was not going to change my confession. To me it was like, if I'm not healed then I'm not saved either, and I might as well throw the Bible out the door. But I knew I *was* saved. And so I knew I *was* healed. In the natural, however, my knee just continued to get worse. It got to the point where even when getting out of bed in the mornings, I had to be careful how I'd move because the pain was so intense. After about one and a half years of this, we received a partner letter from Kenneth Copeland where he wrote, "Be blessed, wise, and in good health!" Shortly after I read it, the Lord said, "Say it!" I did! Some days later, I was invited to go watch some youth play floor hockey at a local gym. As we watched the game, one of the teams happened to need more players. Wearing cowboy boots, I hadn't come prepared to play, but I jumped on the gym floor anyway! I played so hard my face got all red and I was out of breath, seeing as I hadn't been able to exercise like that in so long. Throughout the whole game, playing on a hard floor in boots, I didn't have one single bit of pain in my knee and from that day on I've never had that pain again! And we won the game! Glory to God!

3

IN THE NAME OF JESUS

"But Peter said, 'I do not possess silver and gold, but what I do have I give to you: In the name of Jesus Christ the Nazarene — walk!'"
"And on the basis of faith in His name, it is the name of Jesus which has strengthened this man whom you see and know; and the faith which comes through Him has given him this perfect health in the presence of you all."
Acts 3:6, 16

One might ask, "How does that work, that by simply using the Name of Jesus he gets up healed? Is it that easy?" Yes!

Philippians 2:9 tells us that His name, Jesus, is above every other name! His name supersedes every name that names any kind of sickness, loss, poverty, fear, or pain!

Because of Peter's faith in the power of Jesus' name alone, the Lord was able to bypass all natural means of healing that day!

While faith in His name will sometimes completely bypass natural means, it often works in harmony together with the natural as well.

For example, faith in His name will work to lead you to His perfect wisdom, which when applied in the natural, also secures the victory!

From 2008 - 2014 we visited Juarez, Mexico on multiple occasions. At that time, Juarez was considered one of the most dangerous cities in the world with one of the highest homicide rates, due to intensified drug cartel wars. Fear had gripped so many even in the church, as family members and friends of theirs had also been killed. During one of our visits to a local church there, when I got up to speak, the Lord told me to tell the people to use His NAME!

Rebuke fear in Jesus' name!
Rebuke death in Jesus' name!
Rebuke the crime in Jesus' name!
Declare protection over yourself, your home and property in Jesus' name!

4

ACTION

"And seizing him by the right hand, he raised him up; and immediately his feet and his ankles were strengthened."
Acts 3:7

Unusual action played a dynamic role in completely changing the lame man's daily routine of begging at a gate.

Peter was *full* of the Holy Spirit (Acts 2:4) and *acted* with the Holy Spirit!

Faith is not at a standstill. It moves!

Lip service don't cut it. Faith must *act*!

Shortly before we met a like-minded family who became very close friends, the Lord said to me, "I am putting the doers together; the doers with the doers."

Doubters stay with doubters.

How can two walk together if they don't agree to act?

It is high time to act! For those of us who've had such easy access to an abundance of rich Word preached in the last few decades, if we haven't already done so, it's time to act on what we have heard! If we're saying, "Amen! Hallelujah! Praise the Lord! I agree!", but not acting on it, we are hearers only and not doers.

Acts 3:7 also reminds me of a phrase I once heard from the Lord: "The Fire of Revival and the Boldness of the Holy Spirit." The boldness of Peter and others brought the fire of revival, resulting in 5,000 people being separated from old, religious rule-keeping to new life and grace.

The fire of revival creates an intense hunger for God and righteousness. That desire for what's right, good, and pure, simultaneously and inevitably results in the rejecting of sin and evil.

TESTIMONY

In 2005, I was working at a trailer manufacturer in Texas. I was upstairs at my desk when I heard the Holy Spirit say, "RUN!" I took off down the stairs, opened the door into the workshop, and immediately to my left I saw an employee in danger. He was up on a raised pallet which was holding a huge air compressor. He was trying to steady and counter balance the weight of the compressor as they moved it with a forklift, but it was too heavy for him to control by himself, and he was about to fall with the air compressor on top of him. I called to the forklift driver to stop until I could get up there to help balance the compressor, and we were able to safely move it into its place!

Often, it's the seconds that count. Move when He says move!

5

PRAISE

"With a leap he stood upright and began to walk; and he
entered the temple with them, walking and leaping and
praising God. And all the people saw him
walking and praising God."
Acts 3:8-9

You can praise the Lord, testify, then leap,
OR you can praise the Lord, leap, then testify,
OR you can testify, praise the Lord, then leap,
OR you can testify, leap, then praise the Lord,
OR you can leap, praise the Lord, then testify,
OR you can leap, testify, then praise the Lord!

Let it be seen that we serve a living God! A praise report is fruit,
proving that the Word is true and bringing glory to God!

As Hebrews chapter 11 shows us, having a good report is the
lifestyle of people of faith!

TESTIMONY

In 2001, I was working on a cotton farm in west Texas. One morning after I started the tractor, I just sat there for a while allowing the motor to warm up. Just then the song "Lord, I Hope This Day Is Good" by Don Williams came on the radio. It echoed exactly how I felt that morning - empty, like something was missing. There had to be more. The song became my prayer. It was so big in me that I didn't want to hear anything else and turned the radio off for the day. At lunchtime my brother and I went to the country café in Lenorah, TX, as usual. While there I bumped into one of my friends whom I'd grown up with for about eighteen years on his dad's ranch. I hadn't really seen him in about three years because I'd moved off the ranch onto the cotton farm. He was the kind of guy who, in my religious background and mind, you'd never mention in the same sentence with God. I thought for sure that he and God did not mix! However, as we ate lunch, here he was telling me what God had done and was doing in his life. Although at the time I didn't know what it was, I could feel the anointing all over him and I knew God was in and on him. I felt so small sitting next to him. The willingness of this friend to share his testimony and give God praise is what drove me to dive into the Word of God and to seek God with all my heart, soul, and mind. Since then, I can honestly say I have never lost my hunger for God!

6

POINT TO JESUS

"While he was clinging to Peter and John, all the people ran together to them at the so-called portico of Solomon, full of amazement. But when Peter saw this, he replied to the people, 'Men of Israel, why are you amazed at this, or why do you gaze at us, as if by our own power or piety we had made him walk? The God of Abraham, Isaac and Jacob, the God of our fathers, has glorified His servant Jesus, the one whom you delivered and disowned in the presence of Pilate, when he had decided to release Him.'"
Acts 3:11-13

When the crowd ran together, completely astonished, wondering, "How did this happen?", it created an opportunity to point to Jesus!

Peter *replied*. He opened his mouth and *said* something: "God has glorified His servant Jesus!"

Ecclesiastes 3:7 tells us there is a time to speak and a time to keep silent.

Sometimes the greater mistake is keeping your mouth shut.

Proverbs 15:23 and 25:11 call attention to how *good* and delightful it is to everyone when a timely word and fitting reply are given. It blesses the person who hears it, and brings joy to the person who speaks it!

Over the years, I realized sometimes silence is the dagger thrust rather than a spoken word.

Peter took the opportunity to point to Jesus and *spoke*.

"There is silence until you and I make some noise."

TESTIMONY

In 2002, I went to a prayer meeting at the church I was attending at the time. The Lord had spoken to me in advance, saying He would do one miracle there, but only one, because of their unbelief. There were only a few people at the meeting, but as it turned out I prayed for a man who was well respected in that church. I had no idea anything was wrong with him and all I really remember is that I laid hands on him and prayed in tongues. In the moment, it didn't seem like anything really happened. Several weeks later, his son told me that his dad had told him that the moment I laid hands on his head, he heard a loud popping noise, and that a problem and pain he'd had in his mouth was instantly healed! However, as far as I know he never shared this testimony publicly, nor told me personally. Being the well known and respected man that he was in the church, it would have been a very powerful and impactful opportunity to point the whole community to Jesus and to the healing power of God, and to give God glory! The church would have been quicker to believe him than most. I think the reason he kept quiet was because the supernatural was so strange and foreign to him, especially praying in tongues, that he was afraid to say anything.

7

SIN LIKES THE DARK

"But you disowned the Holy and Righteous One and asked
for a murderer to be granted to you, but put to death the
Prince of life, the one whom God raised from the dead, a
fact to which we are witnesses."
Acts 3:14-15

Those in sin will choose the man in the dark. A corrupt man will
endorse corruption and make sinning easier and more
comfortable for everyone.

How would the hypocritical leaders of the day carry out their lies,
perversion, and evil unchallenged if Jesus was released instead of
a murderer? After all, He would continue to confront their sin just
as He had already been doing!

If a group of friends wants to head out to sin, why would they ask a
righteous buddy to come with them, who might ruin their fun?

The Pharisees' interest in self preservation caused them to disown
one of their own. Remember, this was a mostly religious crowd
who called for Jesus' crucifixion!

Had they even remained in neutral about the idea to condemn Him, but no! In desiring to protect the norm, their ego and we-know-better attitude drove them to actually kill a man who was spotless and without sin!

The dark is not just things like murder or stealing. John 16:8-9 shows us that all sin, which is darkness, begins with simply not believing something God said. Unbelief is the sin that the Holy Spirit came to convict the world of.

Soon after I became truly hungry for Jesus, there was a certain church I would occasionally attend on Sunday evenings. A woman there prophesied to me multiple times, and she was always right on. One time she looked right at me and said, "You will lose friends, because they do not understand the workings of the Holy Spirit, but I will give you Holy Spirit filled friends." And you know something? It's not that my friends weren't saved, but many were just stuck in religious traditions and familiar routine. Their high esteem for family and man far outweighed the excitement of fully following Jesus wherever He may lead. They would rather stay in the darkness of unbelief in some areas so as not to ruffle any feathers. One day during this time, I was at a wedding surrounded by friends from my youth group when I heard the Lord say, "Old wineskins can't handle the new wine." All the tongue-talking, gifts of the Spirit, miracles, signs and wonders were just too much for some of them.

8

FAITH

"And on the basis of faith in His name, it is the name of
Jesus which has strengthened this man whom you see and
know; and the faith which comes through Him has given him
this perfect health in the presence of you all."
Acts 3:16

Without faith it is impossible to please God! (Hebrews 11:6)

How can you not have faith when in the same Bible where it's
written that Jesus paid the price for your sin, it is also written that
He took your sickness and planned life, and life more abundantly,
for you? The same way you receive salvation from sin by faith, is
the exact same way you receive healing, provision, peace,
protection, and every other blessing from God! You simply believe
it in your heart, and speak it with your mouth! (Romans 10:9-10)

Have faith in something bigger than yourself - Jesus! He is the
custodian of your faith. When He says something and you believe
it, He's the one who is responsible to guard and watch over His
Word to make sure it comes to pass!

"Naturally speaking, this won't work."

The voice of God, the Word of God, and the leading of the Holy Spirit must be mixed with faith!

In times past, Peter had not always mixed faith with what Jesus said. Remember, he denied that he even knew Jesus! He didn't have the faith then, but he did now.

"Faith can start at any time."

TESTIMONY

Toward the end of 2002, I began to believe God for a Ford Excursion. I wrote it down, and for a year and a half I would tell people, "God is going to give me a Ford Excursion. I will not pay one penny for it! It'll be white with a gold stripe, and have a good sound system." I told my boss, "When I get it I'll let you drive it around your house!" I'd heard Kenneth E. Hagin preach on Mark 11:23, that you will have what you say, and that's why I was *saying* it. In early 2004, the morning after we got home from our honeymoon, one of my brothers called and said, "I know you often go on missions trips, and now that you're married you'll need a bigger vehicle (I only had a single cab pickup). I saw a Ford Expedition for sale in a nearby town. Do you want to go look at it? I'll buy it for you if you want it." Of course we went and looked at it! It was an Eddie Bauer edition with leather seats, white with a gold stripe (which I had no idea was unique to the Eddie Bauer edition) and a great sound system! Even though I'd been saying I'd have an Excursion, I realized God tweaked my request, because I ended up liking the Expedition a lot more than I would have an Excursion. The next day my brother wrote out the check, paid for tax, title, and license, and we drove our Ford Expedition home!

9

IGNORANCE

"And now, brethren, I know that you acted in ignorance,
just as your rulers did also."
Acts 3:17

Peter stated that a bunch of folk were simply in ignorance when they agreed to have Jesus crucified. Think about it. Jesus, the mediator between heaven and earth was standing in front of them, yet they could not see Him as the One written of in the Old Covenant, nor grasp what He had been doing in that region for the past three years.

Now, after Pentecost, with the help of the Holy Spirit, the church shouldn't miss it so easily.

While still attending the same church I was in when I first got fired up for Jesus, a men's meeting came up. The hot topic concerned two prominent men in the church who were debating whether or not to leave the church. Everyone was giving their opinion about why they should or should not leave. Most did not want them to. It seemed no one was attempting to seek the Lord's view on the matter, remaining ignorant of what He may have to say, because they were so focused on their own opinions. In the middle of the meeting I walked out to get my Bible, because I believed the Lord would lead me to a scripture about the situation. What I received from the Lord to say was: "If there was ever a time to fast and pray about a decision, this would be it. Who wants to argue against the Holy Spirit?" (I understood why God would point out the need to fast in this type of situation, in that fasting helps to crucify the flesh, and the conversation for the most part appeared to be prompted by the flesh.) Nobody else had much more to say after that, and the meeting was soon ended. Outside, a man who later became a pastor there commented to me, "That was wisdom; the wisdom of God!"

One thousand opinions are neutralized when God speaks!

10

PROPHETS

"But the things which God announced beforehand by the
mouth of all the prophets, that His Christ would suffer,
He has thus fulfilled."
"Moses said, 'THE LORD GOD WILL RAISE UP FOR YOU A
PROPHET LIKE ME FROM YOUR BRETHREN; TO HIM YOU
SHALL GIVE HEED to everything He says to you. And it will
be that every soul that does not heed that prophet shall be
utterly destroyed from among the people.' And likewise, all
the prophets who have spoken, from Samuel and his
successors onward, also announced these days. It is you
who are the sons of the prophets and of the covenant which
God made with your fathers, saying to Abraham,
'AND IN YOUR SEED ALL THE FAMILIES OF THE
EARTH SHALL BE BLESSED.'"
Acts 3:18, 22-25

Peter mentions the prophets six times in Acts 3.

In John 16:12, Jesus said He had *many* more things to say. God is
always speaking, and one way He speaks is through the prophets.

In the world, lack of certainty is the norm, but in the church, uncertainty about what's taking place or is coming should not be so prevalent. God has placed in His body the gifts and offices necessary to reveal these things to us.

In the church, we should be talking and hearing about the prophet's office and role as much as we do those of the evangelist, pastor, apostle, and teacher. (Ephesians 4:11)

Ministries, offices, and gifts are like the Carpenter's tools in His toolbox. Whatever it is that needs to be built or fixed, the Lord will use the appropriate tool for the job. However, if we don't understand the tools God has set in the church, or think that some of them have become inactive and unnecessary, we, as a body, will experience a lot more trial and error. It's like having an incomplete blueprint to a house you are building, or trying to build something with a type of tool not designed for that specific task.

Because the background and culture I came from did not understand the prophet's office, the subject was never even mentioned.

I believe some in the church have been called as a prophet, but for reasons such as touched on above, they don't know how to grow or function in it. Maybe they're confused about what a prophet is or does because they have never seen a prophet minister. The fear of man may also hinder them from embracing their calling. To that person I would say: Hey bro! Hey sis! Stick with God. Pray in the Holy Spirit. Walk in love. Forgive. Be real and genuine. Rest. Say what He says when He says to say it.

In Jeremiah chapter 1 we see that one important responsibility of the prophet is to tear down, pluck up, and destroy. Tear down what? The bunch of crap (aka dung, for you Bible scholars) that religion values dearly, when it's simply fluff that man came up with. Read your Bible, dude!

The prophet also plants and builds. They sow the heart of God into your heart, which is the blueprint for the building up of Christ's body.

The prophet speaks the word of the Lord, gives direction, and points out the way.

In 2017, during the night I heard the Lord say, "I am moving prophets back to the forefront." How remarkably we have seen this come to pass, especially in the last year, as we have watched multiple, legit prophets regularly giving the word of the Lord to the whole world. Recent events and new media platforms and shows have served to highlight the prophets' roles at a new level!

11

REPENT, RETURN, REFRESH

"Therefore repent and return, so that your sins may be
wiped away, in order that times of refreshing may come
from the presence of the Lord."
Acts 3:19

To repent and return is your responsibility. The Lord will point,
prompt, guide, reveal, and confirm the way to go, but you and I
still have to choose the path that will lead to times of refreshing.

Repent of what? Repent of acting as the god of your own life. You
can make one hundred years of plans, setting good, positive
goals, but still miss God's perfect plan for your life. Even if you
manage to achieve a degree of success or reach your goals, if
you're not in *His* plan, you will still find yourself feeling empty and
lonely. It's like having a beautiful ring but no wife! However, in
God's plan, He will give you the desires of your heart and you will
be *satisfied* rather than disappointed.

Return to what? Return to the original plan, designed by God for
you long before your mama ever labored to birth you! You carry

the specific, God-given characteristics and talents necessary to fulfill that plan. When you make Jesus the Lord of your life, and get into continual fellowship with Him, you'll begin to see the path.

Refreshment is an inborn human craving. This is why people enjoy getting out into nature! The earth is the Lord's taste, and He created it *for us*. God reveals His nature and makes visible His invisible characteristics through earth's nature. (Romans 1:20) Humanity is divinely drawn to the refreshing that comes from the Lord's presence in Creation. This is one way He speaks to people from the outside in.

I once talked with an inmate who told me that one morning when he had walked out the door to the prison yard, he'd passed a blossoming bush. Just then, the breeze swept the refreshing fragrance up to meet him. That beautiful aroma was what stirred him to believe in the reality of God!

TESTIMONY

Back in the 90's, a construction crew was building a log cabin for the rancher my dad worked for. Working on the ranch part time myself, I got to know the crew somewhat. One of those characters was a foul mouthed, perverted guy. One evening, the friend I'd grown up with on the ranch gave this guy a makeover by cutting his long shaggy hair and shaving his beard, which took multiple razors! This outward change was such a shocking refreshment to him, that it caused him to begin to look at his heart, as to how he could change inwardly as well, which he did shortly after. Days later, as my friend and I were riding down a dirt road he called, relating over the phone how the haircut and shave had changed his life, and all the things God was doing in his life!

12

RETURN OF JESUS

"And that He may send Jesus, the Christ appointed for you, whom heaven must receive until the period of restoration of all things about which God spoke by the mouth of His holy prophets from ancient time."
Acts 3:20-21

Jesus is returning! Jesus is coming back! However, He will not return at just any moment, but at the right moment, when the net is fullest!

Jesus is so compassionate, smart, and brilliant! He knows what He is doing and is working with believers the best He can to cause the greatest number of fish to head toward the net. This is caused by the power of the Gospel!

God absolutely loves humanity whom He created, and has provided a forever relationship with Him. All we have to do is take it!

In 2010, I was in Houston, Texas, with an evangelism group. The team leader announced we'd be meeting at 4:00 am to pray.

When we gathered in the room, the first thing he said was that God had told him He was going to give us a word there during the prayer meeting. I immediately assumed that the Lord would speak through the team leader himself, as He often did, which was pleasant to watch because he was always right on! However, as we prayed in the Holy Spirit, suddenly the Lord spoke through *me*! He said, "Religion and tradition cannot stop Me! Religion and tradition cannot stop My power! It's not part of the Gospel that will be preached and then My return, but it is the *power* of the Gospel that will be preached *first*, to the whole world."

The Lord then impressed on me: Let's say there was a group that had preached salvation from sin through Jesus to the whole world, indisputably the greatest and most important miracle and message. However, if those same people denied the *power* of the Gospel - such as healing, praying in tongues, or the more abundant life message - that is simply not the type of scenario the Lord was referring to when He said the Gospel would be preached to the whole world. They would have preached only *part* of the Gospel, not the *full* Gospel. He's talking about the preaching of that radical bunch who not only preach the good news of salvation, but also the casting out of devils, raising of the dead, supernatural healing, the more abundant lifestyle, the gifts of the Spirit, the baptism of the Holy Spirit, and the anointing! He will not compromise His Word by returning when only *part* of the Gospel has been preached!

In 2002, I was in Eilat, Israel, next to the Red Sea. One morning we were scheduled to go on a boat ride on the Red Sea. The tour group was supposed to be on the boat, ready to go, at a specific time, but a few people were late. The fare was already paid for, and all they had to do was show up, yet some never did. Finally, time was up, the door was shut, and the boat took off. So it will be at the return of Jesus!

13

GOD RAISES PEOPLE UP

"Moses said, 'THE LORD GOD WILL RAISE UP FOR YOU A PROPHET LIKE ME FROM YOUR BRETHREN; TO HIM YOU SHALL GIVE HEED to everything He says to you.'"
"For you first, God raised up His Servant and sent Him to bless you by turning every one of you from your wicked ways."
Acts 3:22, 26

When God raises people up, He separates them from what is common, from opinions, and from religion. He puts them in a place where He can impart the extraordinary into them and where their character is built up.

For example, Moses was in the desert taking care of sheep for 40 years before he had the burning bush experience.

Joseph was thrown in a pit by his own family, sold as a slave, and spent over a decade in prison for a crime he didn't commit. Then, overnight, he was raised to second in command over the entire nation.

David ran for his life, hiding in caves after he had already been anointed as king. Nearly fifteen years passed before he actually took the throne.

After the apostle Paul got saved, he immediately set out for Arabia rather than heading to Jerusalem to hang out with the rest of the apostles. Some may ask, "What was that Lone Ranger doing out there in the desert for three years?" According to Galatians 1 he was receiving revelation from God!

Some people seem to dislike the Lone Ranger! But, why? Isn't he always busting the bad guy and helping the good guy? He and Tonto were radical champs!

The disciples could also have had a who-do-you-think-you-are attitude toward Paul saying, "*We* were the ones who actually, physically spent three years with Jesus! *We* should be teaching *you* a thing or two!" But they didn't.

In all these examples, the Lord showed them how to win and rise above any opposition they faced from either people or the devil. Because they had learned to hear from Him, obey Him only, and walk in victory no matter what, they were ready for the next season of their life.

Remember, there is a difference between separating yourself and God separating you. Some people separate and distance themselves out of rebellion or because they don't want to be near the light that corrects them. God's kind of separation is for the purpose of you being raised up.

In 2008, the Lord spoke to me several times saying, "I'm going to increase you, not decrease you." Soon after, we received direction from Him that, in the natural, appeared to lead us straight into the desert. Looking at it with natural eyes only, it seemed contradictory.

For many years the Lord pointed me to Psalm 4:3 to help me understand why He was separating us from the normal, the expected, and the comfortable. "But know that the Lord has set apart the godly man for Himself." It was so that He Himself could lay some foundations in us without the outside influence of opposing voices. As 11 years in the Psalm 4:3 place began coming to a close, the Lord, referring to that place, said: "There was nobody there to tell you you couldn't do it." Do what? Kill the giant! Did you? Heck, yeah! That's another book!

You see, God does not just separate you *from* something without separating you *to* something. For years I repeatedly heard the Lord say, "Run with the best! Run with the best!" (Proverbs 13:20) It was like a mark set in front of me that made it easy to let go, run on past, leave things behind, and move toward the future. He always wants to increase you, but how can He increase you if you don't first separate from that which decreases you?

KNOWING HIM

Instead of approaching Jesus as though you're walking into a house and leaving the door open behind you so that you can head back out asap, walk in, shut the door behind you, kick off your shoes, and fellowship with Him!

He will say things to you like, "Come to Me, all who are weary and heavy laden, and I will give you rest." (Matthew 11:28)

Maybe you're not sure if you're going to heaven. Maybe you know for sure you're *not*. Saying a cuss word, or lying to your mother in law, or telling your neighbor to go to hell, is not what keeps you out of heaven! What keeps you out is not believing in Jesus. Romans 10:13 says, "Whoever will call on the name of the Lord will be saved."

You are a three part being: spirit, soul, and body. Your spirit is the real you, and when your physical body dies, your spirit will go on to spend eternity in either heaven or hell. If you chose to believe in and call Jesus your Lord, your spirit goes to heaven. If you chose to reject Jesus by not believing in Him, your spirit goes to hell.

As someone who believes in Jesus, it's important to understand that, while your spirit became brand new and perfect the moment you were born again, your mind, which is part of your soul, still needs to be renewed. As long as we're in this physical body here on earth, our minds need to be continuously washed with God's Word, so that our thinking becomes more and more like God's.

If you don't already know Jesus, you can pray something like this:

"Jesus, I want to have eternal life. I believe you died on the cross to pay the penalty for my sins, and that God raised you from the dead. Forgive me of my sins. I forgive all who have done me wrong. Thank you for the gift of eternal life with you! Holy Spirit, fill me to the fullest, and give me a heavenly language to pray in the Spirit (I Corinthians 14:2). Help me to read my Bible, and teach me how to live out my life here on earth."

www.ingramcontent.com/pod-product-compliance
Lightning Source LLC
Chambersburg PA
CBHW071751020426
42331CB00008B/2268